DISNEYLAND PARIS

TRAVEL ADVENTURE GUIDE
2025

MICHELLE A. BROADMAN

A Personal Guide for Your Family's Disneyland Vacation: Expert Tips, Virtual Queue Secrets, Avengers Campus Highlights, Character Meet-and-Greet, Park Rules and Much More!

COPYRIGHT

TIME FOR ADVENTURE

TABLE OF CONTENTS

QUICK VISITOR INFORMATION

What are the hours of operation for Disneyland Paris?

Disneyland Park is open daily from 9:30 am to 10 pm, while Walt Disney Studios Park welcomes visitors daily from 9:30 am to 9 pm. Disney Village operates from 8 am every day. The park is open yearround.

Where is Disneyland Paris located?

★ Disneyland Paris is situated at Bd de Parc, 77700 Coupvray, France.

How many visitors does Disneyland Paris attract each year?

★ The park draws approximately twelve million guests annually.

Does Disneyland Paris offer parking?

★ Guests staying at a Disneyland hotel receive free parking. Paid parking is available near the entrance to Disney Village for other visitors.

★ *Address*: Bd de Parc, 77700 Coupvray, France

★ Disneyland Paris is a sprawling theme park and resort based in Chessy, France. It features two parks—Disneyland Park and Walt Disney Studios Park—along with resort hotels, Disney Nature Resorts, a complex for shopping, dining, and entertainment, and a golf course.

★ *Nearest Landmark*: Golf Paris Val d'Europe

12 FASCINATING FACTS ABOUT DISNEYLAND PARIS

As the only Disney park in Europe since 1992, Disneyland Paris is among the continent's top attractions, captivating visitors from all over the world. Zones like Adventureland, Main Street U.S.A., Fantasyland, Frontierland, Marvel Avengers' Campus, and Toon Studio bring a taste of American wonderland to Europe. However, Disneyland Paris has its own unique charm and character. Here are some interesting facts that make it stand out!

LittleKnown Facts About Disneyland Paris

★ **Secret Tunnels Underneath:** The beloved Disney characters need a way to move between areas without getting caught in crowds. These hidden tunnels allow actors and essential equipment to be transported seamlessly, preserving the magic above ground.

★ **Hidden Mickey Easter Eggs**: Look closely, and you'll find hidden Mickey shapes cleverly incorporated into buildings, decorations, and even weathered spots on treasures. Spotting these subtle surprises is part of the fun!

★ **Listen to Main Street Conversations:** On Main Street, at Market House Deli, an oldfashioned phone booth plays a quirky rotation of "authentic" conversations. Pick up the receiver to enjoy a funny glimpse into the lives of Main Street's "residents."

★ **Real Names on Posters:** The names on posters in the Main Street dentist's window aren't random. They honor key Disney designers—like Jeff Burke and Tom Morris—who brought areas like Discoveryland, Frontierland, and Fantasyland to life.

★ **FrenchInspired Castle with Gold Detail:** Inspired by Europe's historic architecture, Sleeping Beauty's Castle took cues from Mont SaintMichel. The towers are adorned with real 24karat gold leaf, adding a royal touch that's unique to Disneyland Paris.

★ **Stained Glass Crafted by a Master**: English craftsman Paul Chapman, known for his work on Notre Dame, crafted the castle's stained glass in his 80s. Unlike in the film, Snow White's beds here are loaded with treats—a delightful detail for visitors.

★ **Main Street's Real Residents**: Main Street owes much to its "tenants." Storefront windows display names like Walt Disney and his brother Roy as "Founders and Partners." Longtime Disney collaborator Martin Sklar is even listed as the editor of the town newspaper.

★ **Forced Perspective on Main Street:** To make the castle seem farther away, the buildings on Main Street use forced perspective—appearing larger at the base and smaller as they rise. As you head toward the exit, the opposite effect makes it feel closer.

★ **Encounter Local Wildlife**: Disneyland Paris is home to a surprising range of wildlife, including stray cats, which are cared for by staff. Even foxes have been spotted within rides like Peter Pan!

★ **The Park's Color Magic:** With a flash, certain objects reveal hidden colors—one guard will appear pink and another blue, while the raven statue's eyes flash red. The castle itself is designed to photograph beautifully, showcasing impeccable craftsmanship.

★ **Listen for the Beating Heart in the Cemetery:** At Frontierland's Phantom Manor, a large tombstone outside the attraction "beats" in sync with visitors' pulses. Put your ear close to hear it—an eerie detail that adds to the park's spooky charm.

★ **Paris Wasn't the First Choice**: Originally, Disney scouted warmer locations in Europe similar to California and Florida. But Paris won out for its central location, just a short twohour flight from much of Europe.

Disneyland Paris truly combines the magic of Disney with unique European influences, creating a oneofakind experience for all ages.

HOW TO AVOID THE LINES AT DISNEYLAND PARIS

Disneyland Paris is an unforgettable destination, offering a wealth of Disney themed attractions and rides for all ages. Located near Paris, it draws around 12 million visitors annually, making it one of Europe's most popular tourist spots. Here are some tips for avoiding long waits so you can enjoy the magic to the fullest!

Why Skip the Lines at Disneyland Paris?

★ **Avoid Crowds** – As Europe's largest theme park, Disneyland Paris attracts massive crowds. Knowing how to skip lines will help make your visit stressfree.

★ **Save Time** – Popular attractions can have wait times as long as 45 minutes to an hour.

★ **Explore Both Parks Fully** – With over 50 rides and attractions, saving time in line will let you see more of both parks.

★ **More Time for MeetandGreets** – Cutting down wait times allows extra time to interact with your favorite Disney characters.

How to Avoid the Lines at Disneyland Paris

Buy Tickets Online

★ Save time by purchasing tickets in advance. Book online to avoid lengthy ticketcounter lines and enter the parks more smoothly.

Stay at a Disneyland Hotel

★ Guests at Disneyland Paris hotels enjoy perks like early park access (Extra Magic Time) before regular opening hours.

Hotel stays also include free parking and sometimes ticket discounts, letting you make the most of your visit.

Arrive Early

★ Visiting during the park's opening hours means smaller crowds and shorter lines. Arriving early lets you explore more freely and even enjoy oneonone time with characters like Mickey Mouse and the princesses.

Stay Until Closing

★ As closing time nears, many visitors leave, so lines are shorter. This is a great chance to enjoy rides in the evening glow and make memories under the lights of Disneyland Paris.

Use Disney Premier Access

★ Premier Access offers priority access to select attractions. Purchase it through the Disneyland Paris app or at the park. Note that this addon works with both parks and lets you skip lines at specific rides during set time slots.

Opt for the Single Rider Line

★ The Single Rider option allows solo visitors to enter rides faster. Although you may not sit with your group, this free service lets you experience more attractions with minimal wait.

Visitor Tips

★ **Ideal Times to Visit:** The best times are early morning and just before closing.

- ★ **Book Premier Access**: This can be reserved on the app for popular attractions like Indiana Jones and the Temple of Peril or Phantom Manor.
- ★ **Stay at a Disney Hotel**: For a full experience, a 23 day stay is recommended. Hotel guests get Extra Magic Time and ticket discounts.
- ★ **PreBook Dining**: Many Disney restaurants book up to two months in advance, so reserve a table to avoid disappointment.
- ★ **Use Rider Switch:** This service lets parents take turns on adult rides without waiting twice in line, making it easier for families with young children.

WHY VISIT DISNEYLAND PARIS

- ★ Meet Iconic Characters – From Disney princesses to Marvel superheroes, enjoy meetandgreets and parades.
- ★ Multiple Themes in One Place With themes like Pirates of the Caribbean and Cars, there's something for everyone.
- ★ Exciting Rides, whether thrilling or gentle, Disneyland Paris has rides to suit all tastes.
- ★ Fun Shows and Festivals Join in festive events like the Christmas parade or Halloween celebration.
- ★ Shops and Dining – Explore themed shops, eateries, and even a 27hole golf course!

- ★ Character Dining and Fireworks
- ★ Enjoy meals with your favorite characters, and end your night with a magical fire works show.

DISNEYLAND PARIS FACILITIES

Services for Adults, Children, and Guests with Disabilities

Disneyland Paris provides extensive facilities to ensure a comfortable and magical experience for everyone, including adults, children, individuals with disabilities, and even pets.

★ Hotels

Guests can choose from various themed Disney hotels for a complete experience. You can choose between Disney Newport Bay Club, Disney Hotel Santa Fe, and Disney Sequoia Lodge on the property. Resort guests also benefit from ticket discounts and park proximity.

★ Restaurants

From Parisian to Caribbean cuisine, Disneyland Paris offers a variety of dining options. There are also vegetarian and veganfriendly dishes to cater to diverse preferences.

★ Guest Services

Disneyland Paris offers services such as First Aid, drinking water fountains, Disney Check (nutritional information), and free WiFi across the park.

★ Defibrillators (AEDs)

Automated External Defibrillators are available throughout the park to address cardiac emergencies. Guests can always find AEDs using the guide map or by asking a Cast Member around.

★ First Aid

The park has First Aid centers available daily, staffed by qualified personnel. They also offer facilities for storing medications requiring refrigeration. First Aid stations operate on the following schedule:

- Disneyland Park: 7 AM to 2 hours after closing.
- Walt Disney Studio: Note that they open 30 minutes before the park opens.
- Disney Village: 2 PM to 12:30 AM.

★ Water Fountains

Guests can stay hydrated with water fountains located throughout the park. Use the Disneyland Paris app or map for easy access to these locations.

★ Letterboxes

Disneyland Paris has letterboxes throughout the park, so guests can send postcards and letters. Stamps are available at Disney shops.

★ ATMs

Several Crédit Mutuel ATMs are available throughout the park for convenient cash withdrawals.

★ WiFi

Guests can connect to free WiFi across the Disneyland Paris parks, hotels, and Disney Village, making it easy to stay connected and access the Disneyland app.

★ Parking

Disneyland Paris offers a car park with the following fees:

- Cars (under 2m): €30
- Vehicles (over 2m): €30
- Campervans: €45
- Motorbikes: €25

Disney hotel guests and Annual Pass holders can enjoy free parking, with some exceptions during special events.

★ Portable Charging Rental

Charging rentals are available for keeping devices powered. Options include fullycharged power banks with various adapters.

★ Restrooms and Baby Care Centers

Accessible restrooms with babychanging tables are available throughout the park. Baby Care Centers provide changing rooms, microwaves for heating food, and breastfeeding areas.

★ Pushchair and Wheelchair Rentals

Strollers and wheelchairs are available at Town Square Terrace near the Disneyland Park entrance for a fee.

★ Animal Care Centre

For guests with pets, the Animal Care Centre provides care while guests are in the park. Guests must supply food for their pets.

★ Lost & Found

Lost items can be reported and retrieved at the Lost and Found center located at City Hall in Disneyland Park.

★ Smoking Areas

Smoking is restricted to designated outdoor areas within the park.

★ Accessibility Services for Guests with Disabilities

Disneyland Paris offers numerous accessibility services to ensure that all guests can enjoy the park.

★ Accessibility Map

This map highlights services for guests with disabilities, including accessible restrooms, stroller/wheelchair rentals, and parking.

★ Audio Description Services

The AudioSpot app helps visually impaired guests navigate attractions, restaurants, and theaters. Guests should bring their own hearing aids and chargers.

★ Guide and Assistance Dogs

Assistance dogs are welcome, though they must be leashed and have uptodate documents. These dogs are allowed in gardens but not on rides so you don't get frightened.

★ Stroller & Wheelchair Rentals

Guests can rent wheelchairs and pushchairs near the entrance at Town Square Terrace in Disneyland Park. The Accessibility Map provides more information on rental centers.

Disneyland Paris provides an inclusive environment with dedicated facilities and services, ensuring an enjoyable experience for all guests.

DISNEY VILLAGE

- ★ **Official Name**: Disney Village
- ★ **Opening Date**: April 12, 1992
- ★ **Operating Hours**: 8 AM to 12 AM
- ★ **Location**: MarnelaVallée, France
- ★ **Owner**: The Walt Disney Company
- ★ **Annual Visitors**: 12 million
- ★ **Area**: 18,000 square meters
- ★ Purpose: Shopping, dining, and entertainment hub
- ★ Popular Attractions: Disney Village Cinemas, Rainforest Cafe, Planet Hollywood, World of Disney

Disney Village sits in MarnelaVallée, France, nestled between Disneyland Park, Walt Disney Studios Park, and the Disney Hotels. If you're staying at a Disney Hotel, you can reach Disney Village by taking the complimentary Disneyland Paris shuttle service, which operates every 12 minutes, seven days a week, from 6:30 AM to 11 PM.

Please note that the shuttle service does not stop at Disney's Davy Crockett Ranch, Villages Nature Paris, Golf Disneyland, or Disneyland Hotel. For those staying at Villages Nature Paris, there is a public shuttle bus option.

TOP THINGS TO DO AT DISNEY VILLAGE

Entertainment at Disney Village

Web Radio: Tune into Disney Village Web Radio any time of day for a mix of jazz, Disney classics, and more. It also keeps you updated on events, musical performances, and live shows happening throughout Disney Village Paris.

Gaumont Cinemas: Enjoy animated blockbusters, romantic comedies, and Disney classics at the Gaumont Cinema. The theater's neon decor and vintage aesthetic bring an '80s vibe to its 15 screens. With the IMAX Laser system, your movie experience will be even more captivating. Check showtimes ahead of your visit to plan your movie viewing.

PanoraMagique: Soar above Disneyland Paris for a 360° view on one of the world's largest tethered hot air balloons. This 6minute helium balloon ride, anchored on Lake Disney, gives you panoramic views as far as 20 km on clear days.

Stadium: Step back to the '90s with hightech arcade games at the Stadium. This familyfriendly arcade is packed with dance machines, driving simulators, and classic games for all ages.

EVENTS AT DISNEY VILLAGE

Halloween at Disneyland Paris

Halloween is a fantastic time to visit Disneyland Paris, with the park adorned in festive Halloween decor and plenty of spooky activities to enjoy. Special events and themed attractions fill the park from October 1 to November 5, 2024.

Operating Hours During Halloween

- Monday to Friday: 9:30 am 9 pm
- Saturday and Sunday: 9:30 am 10 pm
- October 29 to 31: 9:30 am 2 am

Disneyland Paris Halloween todo list

- Embrace the Spooky Atmosphere
- Enjoy the festive decorations, from grinning pumpkins to friendly ghosts, and costumed characters throughout the parks. There's a mix of spooky and familyfriendly events and attractions for everyone.
- Indulge in Halloween Treats
- Sample special Halloween treats, apple cider stations, and candies throughout the park. There's also a haunted house, trickortreating zones, and fireworks displays for extra fun.
- Shop for Halloween Souvenirs
- Find Halloweenthemed souvenirs like Mickey Mouse ears and other spooky items at Disneyland Paris shops. From

lighthearted keepsakes to collectible shirts, there's something to remember the season by.

Visitor Tips

If you're planning a visit in October 2025, it's best to book tickets early, as Halloween season is quite popular. Bring sunscreen and suitable clothing for varied autumn weather, with temperatures between 17°C and 10°C. Note that Halloween parties from October 29 to 31 are ticketed events and may not be ideal for young children as they run late and can be quite dark. Costumes are allowed, but please avoid costume weapons and posing as Disney characters for autographs.

OVERVIEW OF FRANCE

Welcome to France, a country where history, culture, and natural beauty come together to create unforgettable experiences. Exploring the bustling streets of Paris, the serene vineyards of Bordeaux, or the stunning coastline of the French Riviera, is something every traveler should experience. This guide aims to provide detailed and practical information to make your trip as exciting and enjoyable as possible. This is just a little rundown before we go into the focus of attraction which is Disneyland Theme Parks.

GETTING THERE AND AROUND

- **Air Travel**: France is wellconnected internationally, with major airports in Paris (Charles de Gaulle and Orly), Nice, Lyon, and Marseille. Many cities in the United States offer direct flights. Once you arrive, highspeed trains (TGV) and a welldeveloped domestic flight network make it easy to travel within the country.

- **Public Transportation**: The French public transportation system is efficient and userfriendly. In cities, you'll find extensive metro, tram, and bus networks. Paris, for example, has one of the most comprehensive metro systems in the world. For longer distances, the TGV trains can whisk you across the country at speeds up to 200 mph.

- **Car Rentals**: Renting a car offers excellent flexibility for your travels. French roads are generally in excellent condition, and the scenic drives through regions like Provence and the Loire Valley are not to be missed. Be aware of the tolls on major highways and consider a GPS or a reliable map.

WHERE TO STAY

Paris: The capital offers a range of accommodations from luxury hotels to budgetfriendly hostels. The Marais district is perfect for those who love history and boutique shopping, while Montmartre provides a bohemian atmosphere with incredible views of the city.

- **Provence**: Staying in a traditional Provençal farmhouse or a charming bed and breakfast can add a unique touch to your experience. Cities like Avignon and AixenProvence are ideal bases for exploring the region.
- **French Riviera:** If you're heading to the coast, Nice offers a blend of city and sea with plenty of hotels and guesthouses. For a more glamorous stay, consider the opulent resorts of Cannes or SaintTropez.

Exploring Paris

- **The Eiffel Tower**: No trip to Paris is complete without visiting its most iconic landmark. You can take the elevator or, for the more adventurous, climb the stairs to the second level for a spectacular view of the city.
- **Louvre Museum**: Home to thousands of works of art, including the Mona Lisa and the Venus de Milo, the Louvre is a mustvisit. Plan to spend at least a halfday here to truly appreciate its vast collections.
- **NotreDame Cathedral:** Despite the devastating fire in 2019, the cathedral remains a symbol of Gothic architecture. You can still view the exterior and see the progress of the restoration work.
- **Seine River Cruise:** A leisurely boat ride along the Seine offers a unique perspective of Paris's landmarks. Always go

for an evening cruise to see how beautifully the city is illuminated.

The Charm of Provence

Lavender Fields: Visit during the summer months to see the fields in full bloom. The most famous fields are located in the Luberon and near the town of Sault.

Avignon: Known for the stunning Palais des Papes, Avignon is a city rich in history and culture. The annual Avignon Festival in July is one of the most important events in the European theater calendar.

Gorges du Verdon: Often referred to as Europe's Grand Canyon, this natural wonder offers opportunities for hiking, kayaking, and rock climbing. The turquoise waters and dramatic cliffs make it a breathtaking destination.

The Glamour of the French Riviera

Nice: Stroll along the Promenade des Anglais, relax on the pebbled beaches, or explore the vibrant Old Town. Nice is a city that combines relaxation with culture.

Cannes: Known for its film festival, Cannes also offers luxury shopping, fine dining, and beautiful beaches. Take a walk along the Boulevard de la Croisette to experience its glitzy atmosphere.

Monaco: A short drive from Nice, the principality of Monaco is famous for its casino, the royal palace, and the Grand Prix. It's a place where luxury and history meet.

WINE AND CUISINE

Bordeaux: Explore the worldrenowned vineyards of Bordeaux, where you can tour châteaux and sample some of the best wines in the world. The city itself is also a UNESCO World Heritage site with beautiful architecture and a vibrant food scene.

Burgundy: Known for its Pinot Noir and Chardonnay, Burgundy offers picturesque vineyards and charming villages. Don't miss the town of Beaune, the wine capital of the region.

French Cuisine: From croissants and baguettes to coq au vin and crème brûlée, French cuisine is celebrated worldwide. Take the time to enjoy a leisurely meal at a local bistro or indulge in a fine dining experience at a Michelinstarred restaurant.

PRACTICAL TIPS

Language: While French is the official language, you'll find that many people in the tourist industry speak English. Mastering a few basic French phrases can enrich your experience and is often warmly received by locals.

Currency: France uses the Euro (€). Credit cards are widely accepted, but it's always good to have some cash on hand for smaller purchases and in more rural areas.

Travel Insurance: It's wise to have comprehensive travel insurance that covers health, accidents, and travel disruptions.

Emergency Numbers: The emergency number in France is 112, which can be dialed for police, medical, and fire emergencies.

France is a country that offers a wealth of experiences, from its bustling cities to its serene countryside. Whether you're an art lover, a history buff, or simply looking to enjoy the finer things in life, France has something to offer. This guide to help plan your trip and make the most of your time in this incredible country as it will be focusing on the Adventurous Theme Park of Paris.

CHAPTER 1

OVERVIEW OF DISNEYLAND PARIS

Welcome to Disneyland Paris, a land where people often imagine and storytelling come to life against the backdrop of French charm and classic Disney magic. Situated just 20 miles east of central Paris in MarnelaVallée, Disneyland Paris is much more than just a theme park—it's a carefully crafted world of fantasy, adventure, and nostalgia. Here, you'll find two distinct parks, Disneyland Park and Walt Disney Studios Park, each with its own set of attractions, shows, and themed lands. Opened in 1992, Disneyland Paris has become Europe's top tourist destination, drawing in millions of visitors each year who come to experience the beloved characters, thrilling rides, and rich cultural touches unique to this location.

Disneyland Paris isn't just a European replica of its American counterparts. It carries its own unique personality, blending Disney magic with European artistry and storytelling. Once you are into the park, you'll notice the attention to detail in every structure and space, from the whimsical streets of Main Street, U.S.A. to the mysterious ruins of Adventureland and the futuristic attractions of Discoveryland. Each corner of the park is designed to transport you to a different time and place, making it a truly unique Disney experience.

Disneyland Park

This is the park that will feel familiar to those who have visited other Disney resorts, but with its own distinctive European flair. Spread across five themed lands, Disneyland Park is home to the iconic Sleeping Beauty Castle, the first you'll see with a truly European medieval style, inspired by France's fairytale castles and Gothic architecture.

Each themed land offers something for everyone.

Main Street, U.S.A. transports you to early 20thcentury America, with gaslit street lamps, horsedrawn streetcars, and buildings that look like they came straight out of a small American town. Here, you'll find shops filled with unique souvenirs and restaurants serving up classic American fare. As you stroll down the street, take a moment to look around at the meticulous attention to period detail, from vintage signage to the soft strains of jazz music playing in the background.

Fantasyland brings beloved fairytales to life. With whimsical rides like Peter Pan's Flight and Alice's Curious Labyrinth, this is where dreams meet reality. The land's focal point is the majestic Sleeping Beauty Castle, where you can explore a gallery of beautiful stainedglass windows telling the tale of Sleeping Beauty. Kids and adults alike will love the magic woven into every corner, from the storybook cottages to the intricate sculptures depicting beloved characters.

Adventureland invites you to explore exotic locales, from the mysterious jungles of Indiana Jones and the Temple of Peril to the bustling marketplace of an Arabian bazaar. This is the land of daring escapades and hidden treasures, where you'll find one of Disneyland Paris's most iconic rides, Pirates of the Caribbean, which offers a grand journey through pirateinfested waters, packed with detailed scenes and memorable characters.

Frontierland takes you to the rugged Wild West, with its dusty trails, wooden saloons, and the thrilling Big Thunder Mountain Railroad, a roller coaster set on a runaway mine train that winds through canyons and cliffs. Here, you'll feel the spirit of adventure and discovery that defined the American frontier, complete with rustic décor and dramatic rock formations that set the scene.

Discoveryland is Disneyland Paris's nod to the future, with a retrofuturistic twist. Inspired by the vision of great thinkers like Jules Verne, Discoveryland offers attractions like Hyperspace Mountain, a highspeed journey through the galaxy, and Buzz Lightyear Laser Blast, where you can team up with Buzz Lightyear himself to take down Emperor Zurg.

WALT DISNEY STUDIOS PARK IN PARIS

Opened in 2002, Walt Disney Studios Park is located in MarnelaVallée, France, about 20 miles from the center of Paris.

As one of two parks in Disneyland Paris, this park is centered around showbiz, film themes, behindthescenes filmmaking, and immersive Disney animation. It offers a fresh Disney experience through imaginative themes inspired by beloved Disney stories.

In 2022, the park unveiled the Avengers Campus, adding even more attractions. Expansion plans also include new areas dedicated to Frozen and Star Wars.

Why Visit Walt Disney Studios Park?

- **Step into the movies**: Movie enthusiasts will love Walt Disney Studios Park, with attractions like the Twilight Zone Tower of Terror and Star Tours: The Adventures Continue, making you feel like you're part of the films.
- **Meet beloved characters**: Mickey Mouse, Minnie Mouse, Donald Duck, and more await visitors in person at the park.
- **Experience Disney's magic:** With magical parades and stunning fireworks shows, you'll feel transported to another world.

- **Discover the art of filmmaking**: The Backlot Tour reveals the process of moviemaking, and the Animation Academy offers lessons in drawing your favorite characters.
- **Family fun for everyone**: With rides, shows, and attractions for all ages, the whole family can enjoy a day filled with fun.

Timings

- Open daily from 9:30 am to 9 pm.

Extra Magic Time:

- Guests staying at Disneyland Paris hotels and annual pass holders get early entry from 8:30 am to 9:30 am.

Best time to visit:

MidJanuary to midMay and September offer pleasant weather. Visiting on weekdays, especially Tuesday through Thursday, helps avoid long lines and crowds.

Front Lot

At the entrance of Walt Disney Studios Park, the Front Lot celebrates filmmaking. The boulevard here is inspired by Hollywood Boulevard in Los Angeles. Stroll through this area to discover the secrets behind famous Hollywood sets and immerse yourself in the world of cinema.

Production Courtyard

This area is full of exciting rides, shows, and dining options, with a 1950s American TV show theme. You can also enjoy tours that reveal moviemaking secrets, live performances, and chances to meet your favorite Disney characters and superheroes.

Toon Studio

Toon Studio is the park's largest area, where the magic of animation comes to life. Explore memorable moments and characters from Disney, Pixar, Marvel, and more. Special holiday performances include Mickey Mouse and the Magician and Mickey's Christmas Big Band.

Worlds of Pixar

Worlds of Pixar transports you into scenes from beloved films like Finding Nemo, Ratatouille, Toy Story, and Cars. Enjoy rides, themed dining, and vibrant attractions that let you experience these iconic stories.

The Marvel Avengers Campus

This Marvelthemed campus opened on July 20, 2022, offering a highly immersive superhero experience. Join Avengers Assemble: Flight Force or SpiderMan W.E.B Adventure, and look out for Avengers like Thor, who might recruit you for a mission. Refuel at themed restaurants like Stark Factory and PYM Kitchen.

WALT DISNEY STUDIOS PARK HISTORY

Initially planned as DisneyMGM Studios Park and set to open in 1995, the project was delayed due to financial constraints, eventually opening on March 16, 2002.

In June 2007, an animation courtyard was introduced, showcasing Disney's animated characters with unique rides, meetandgreets, and merchandise. By 2009, the park offered new shows like Playhouse Disney – Live on Stage! in three languages and the Disney's Cinema Parade, inspired by popular Disney films.

In 2018, a multiyear transformation was announced in preparation for the 2024 Olympics. This phase, with a 2 billion Euro budget, features expansions focused on Marvel, Star Wars, and Frozen.

HISTORY AND EVOLUTION

Disneyland Paris has a story that stretches back to the 1980s, when The Walt Disney Company began looking to expand its reach internationally. Having successfully opened parks in California and Florida, Disney set its sights on Europe, where the magic of Disney films and characters was already deeply loved. Out of several possible locations, including Spain, the French region of MarnelaVallée was chosen due to its proximity to Paris and its central location within Western Europe, making it accessible to millions of potential visitors. However, this decision was met with both excitement and controversy, leading to a journey of cultural adaptation, challenges, and ultimately, success.

The Early Years

Disneyland Paris, originally known as Euro Disney Resort, opened its doors on April 12, 1992. The launch was met with much anticipation, but also a degree of skepticism, especially from locals and critics who worried that American culture might overshadow French traditions. The park's initial years were marked by financial struggles, as visitor numbers were lower than expected, and the project faced cultural resistance. From the Americanstyle food offered in the park to a perceived overemphasis on the "American way" of theme park entertainment, many French residents believed that Euro Disney didn't align with their beliefs and preferences. Despite its beautiful design and ambitious attractions, the park struggled to find its footing.

Disney quickly realized that some adjustments were necessary to appeal to the European audience. For instance, more wine options were added to the dining venues, and the overall dining experience was revamped to reflect a blend of French and international cuisine. Disney also worked on improving relationships with the local community, promoting the park as a celebration of both American innovation and European artistry. Over time, these changes started to pay off as visitors grew more comfortable with the idea of a Disney park in France.

Rebranding and the Transition to Disneyland Paris

In 1994, the park was rebranded from Euro Disney Resort to Disneyland Paris, signaling a new phase focused on bridging Disney's identity with its European setting. This rebranding came with several structural and operational changes that helped the park find a stronger connection with both French visitors and tourists from across Europe. The park also gained support from the French government, which saw its potential as a major tourist destination that could boost the local economy.

During this period, Disneyland Paris began to gain popularity, especially among young families and Disney fans who appreciated the unique charm of a Disney park set in Europe. The rebranding wasn't just about the name it symbolized Disney's commitment to honoring local cultures while still offering the fantasy and wonder associated with its brand. By the late 1990s, Disneyland Paris had found a better rhythm, becoming more culturally attuned and financially stable.

Expansion and the Opening of Walt Disney Studios Park

As visitor numbers grew, Disneyland Paris began planning its first major expansion. In 2002, a second park, Walt Disney Studios Park, opened to offer guests a behindthescenes look at the world of film, animation, and television. This addition expanded the resort into a multipark destination, much like Disneyland in California or Walt Disney World in Florida. Walt Disney Studios Park introduced attractions like The Twilight Zone Tower of Terror and, more recently, Ratatouille: The Adventure, an attraction inspired by the beloved Pixar film set in Paris.

Walt Disney Studios Park allowed Disneyland Paris to diversify its attractions, offering experiences that appealed not only to fans of classic Disney characters but also to those who enjoyed thrill rides and filmthemed attractions. While it initially opened with fewer attractions than planned, the park has gradually expanded and continues to grow, with exciting new lands and attractions that are transforming it into a major draw for visitors.

Overcoming Financial Challenges and Gaining Popularity

Despite its growing popularity, Disneyland Paris faced significant financial challenges over the years. High construction costs, debt, and occasional dips in attendance led to financial restructuring. In 2017, The Walt Disney Company took full control of Disneyland Paris, buying out the remaining shares from European investors. This move allowed Disney to invest more heavily in park improvements, entertainment offerings, and future expansions, with plans for major additions like Marvel, Star Wars, and Frozenthemed areas.

The decision to fully integrate Disneyland Paris into The Walt Disney Company's operations marked a turning point for the resort. With new investments, fresh ideas, and a commitment to enhancing the guest experience, Disneyland Paris began to flourish, attracting more visitors from across Europe and beyond.

Recent Developments and Looking Ahead

Today, Disneyland Paris is a thriving resort that welcomes over 10 million visitors each year. The park continues to evolve, adding new attractions, seasonal events, and themed lands. One of the most anticipated projects is the expansion of Walt Disney Studios Park, which will include areas dedicated to Frozen and Marvel superheroes, along with a new lake that will host nighttime shows and entertainment.

In 2024, Disneyland Paris reopened its flagship hotel, the Disneyland Hotel, after a major renovation. This luxurious property now features royalthemed decor inspired by Disney Princesses, creating an experience fit for both adults and children who want a taste of Disney's storytelling within a European luxury setting.

Looking forward, Disneyland Paris has ambitious plans to remain a worldclass destination. Its continued expansion, combined with a deeper understanding of European tastes and preferences, has positioned it as a unique Disney park that celebrates its surroundings while delivering the magical experiences Disney is known for. Disneyland Paris has not only survived the early challenges but has emerged as a beloved destination.

Disneyland Paris stands today as a testament to the power of adaptation and resilience. It has grown from its humble and somewhat rocky beginnings into a cherished resort that blends Disney's storytelling with French culture. The park's evolution is a fascinating journey of cultural blending, creativity, and perseverance, making it a unique Disney experience that celebrates both its roots and its future.

Disneyland Paris offers a unique blend of classic Disney magic with a distinctly European touch, making it an unmatched destination for all ages. situated just outside Paris, this worldrenowned resort combines the thrill and wonder of iconic Disney experiences with the rich culture and elegance France is famous for.

For families, couples, and solo adventurers alike, Disneyland Paris provides an opportunity to experience favorite characters and attractions up close, with added details that celebrate the park's European roots. The castle here isn't just any castle; it's Sleeping Beauty Castle, inspired by French Gothic architecture and even featuring a dragon's lair in its depths—something unique to Disneyland Paris. This park doesn't simply recreate American Disney parks but instead adds layers that reflect local culture, art, and storytelling traditions.

Disneyland Paris also brings a seasonal variety to its celebrations, marking events like Halloween and Christmas with grand decorations, themed shows, and even tailored menus across the park. Fans of Disney films will find that Disneyland Paris showcases European influences in its storytelling, from the Renaissanceinspired artwork to live entertainment that pays tribute to both French history and Disney classics.

The park is also conveniently connected to central Paris, so visitors can blend a Disney adventure with sightseeing in one of the world's most beloved cities. Within a 45minute journey, guests can go from meeting Mickey Mouse to admiring the Eiffel Tower—a unique feature that makes Disneyland Paris a wellrounded destination.

Ultimately, Disneyland Paris isn't just a stop on the global map of Disney parks; it's a thoughtfully designed experience that invites visitors to enjoy Disney magic with a special European flair.

60 Perks and Hacks to Enhance Your Disney Experience:

Planning and Booking

- Use a Disney Travel Agent : They can help you find deals and handle reservations, often at no extra cost.
- Book Dining Reservations Early : Reservations open 60 days in advance; popular spots fill up quickly.

- Stay at a Disney Resort : Enjoy perks like early park entry and complimentary transportation.
- Visit During OffPeak Seasons : Experience lower crowds and potentially better rates.
- Purchase Tickets in Advance : Save money and time by buying tickets before arriving at the park.

Park Navigation and Timing

- Arrive Early for Rope Drop : Be among the first to enter and enjoy shorter lines.
- Stay Late : Crowds thin out near closing time, offering shorter waits.
- Use Single Rider Lines : Available on select attractions for quicker access.
- Plan a Midday Break : Avoid peak crowds and heat by resting during the afternoon.
- Utilize Park Hopper Tickets : Visit multiple parks in a single day for more flexibility.

Dining and Food

- Mobile Order Meals : Use the app to order food in advance and skip lines.
- Share Meals : Portions are generous; sharing can save money and reduce waste.

- Bring Snacks and Water : Save money and stay hydrated by bringing your own.
- Ask for Free Water : Counterservice restaurants provide complimentary cups of water.
- Try Unique Treats : Each park offers exclusive snacks worth exploring.

Attractions and Entertainment

- Use Genie+ and Lightning Lane : Access shorter lines for popular rides.
- Check Showtimes in Advance : Plan your day around mustsee performances.
- Experience Less Popular Attractions During Peak Times : Shorter lines for shows and rides.
- Watch Parades from Less Crowded Areas : Find spots with fewer people for a better view.
- Enjoy Nighttime Shows from Unique Locations : Some areas offer great views with less crowding.

- **Technology and Apps**
- Download the My Disney Experience App : Essential for maps, wait times, and reservations.
- Enable Notifications : Stay updated on reservation times and park alerts.

- Use Disney's Free WiFi : Available throughout the parks to save on data.
- Bring a Portable Charger : Keep devices powered for photos and app usage.
- Set Up Mobile Payments : Link a card for quick and contactless transactions.

CostSaving Tips

- Buy Disney Gift Cards at a Discount : Retailers like Target offer discounts on gift cards.
- Bring Your Own Poncho : Avoid buying expensive ones in the park.
- Use Refillable Popcorn Buckets : Purchase once and get cheap refills.
- Take Advantage of Free Activities : Enjoy parades, fireworks, and character meetandgreets without extra cost.
- Look for Package Deals : Bundling hotel, tickets, and dining can offer savings.

Health and Comfort

- Wear Comfortable Shoes : Expect extensive walking; supportive footwear is crucial.
- Stay Hydrated : Carry a water bottle and refill throughout the day.

- Apply Sunscreen Regularly : Protect your skin from prolonged sun exposure.
- Take Breaks in AirConditioned Areas : Shops and indoor attractions offer a cool respite.
- Use Baby Care Centers : Available for feeding, changing, and resting with young children.

Special Experiences

- Celebrate Special Occasions : Inform cast members for potential surprises.
- Participate in Interactive Games : Games like Sorcerers of the Magic Kingdom add extra fun
- Attend Seasonal Events : Festivals and holiday parties offer unique experiences.
- Book BehindtheScenes Tours : Gain insight into park operations and history.
- Try Resort Hopping : Explore different Disney resorts for dining and entertainment.

Merchandise and Souvenirs

- Shop Early or Late : Stores are less crowded at opening and closing.
- Send Purchases to Your Hotel : Available for Disney resort guests to avoid carrying items.

- Look for Unique Items : Each park and resort offers exclusive merchandise.
- Collect Pressed Pennies : Affordable souvenirs available throughout the parks.
- Use Disney Gift Cards : Manage spending by loading a set amount for souvenirs.

Transportation and Logistics

- Use Disney Transportation : Buses, monorails, and boats are free for guests.
- Check Transportation Schedules : Plan your day around transit times.
- Consider Ride Sharing Services : For quicker travel between parks or resorts.
- Arrive Early for Parking : Get better spots and avoid long walks.
- Know Park Opening Procedures : Some areas open before official times.

Miscellaneous Tips

- Bring a Small Backpack : Carry essentials without being cumbersome.
- Label Your Stroller : Make it easily identifiable among many others.

- Use Rider Switch : Allows parents to take turns on rides without double waiting.

CHAPTER 2

PLANNING YOUR TRIP

Best Times to Visit

Budgeting and Costs

Choosing the Right Ticket Type

Essential Apps and Resources for Planning

Transportation Tips on How to Get to Disneyland Paris

Best Times to Visit

Here's the trick, choosing the ideal time to visit Disneyland Paris can greatly enhance your experience. The park is open all year, but different seasons offer varied experiences and you should take that into great consideration.

Spring (April to June): This period brings mild weather and blooming gardens, making it a pleasant time to visit. Crowds are moderate, and the park often hosts springthemed events.

Summer (July to August): The busiest time of year, with long park hours and additional entertainment. Expect larger crowds and higher prices, but the warm weather is perfect for enjoying all the outdoor attractions.

Fall (September to October): The weather cools down, and crowds lessen. Halloween decorations and events add a festive atmosphere to the parks.

Winter (November to March): The offpeak season sees fewer visitors, except during the Christmas and New Year holidays. The park transforms with holiday decorations and special winter events, offering a magical experience despite the cold weather.

Budgeting and Costs

Planning a budget for Disneyland Paris involves several key aspects like the following;

Tickets: Prices fluctuate based on the season and type of ticket. Singleday tickets for adults range from €50 to €100, while multiday passes offer better value for extended stays.

Accommodation: Onsite hotels range from luxury options to budgetfriendly choices, with nightly rates between €100 and €600. Nearby offsite accommodations may provide more affordable options.

Food and Drink: Account for meals and snacks within the park. Quickservice meals typically cost around €10, while character dining and other themed restaurants can be €60 or more.

Travel: Factor in the cost of transportation to and from the park. Options include flights to Paris, train travel, or car rentals.

Extras: Remember to budget for souvenirs, special events, and addons like Disney Premier Access to make the most of your visit.

Choosing the Right Ticket Type

Disneyland Paris offers a variety of ticket options to suit different needs and preferences:

SingleDay Tickets: Ideal for those with limited time. Prices vary based on the date of visit.

MultiDay Tickets: Great for extended stays, allowing you to explore both parks over several days.

Annual Passes: Perfect for frequent visitors, offering numerous benefits such as discounts, special event access, and unlimited visits.

Undated Tickets: Provide flexibility to visit on any date, perfect for those who prefer an open schedule.

Essential Apps and Resources for Planning

Several tools and resources can enhance your Disneyland Paris experience:

Official Disneyland Paris App: This app provides realtime information on wait times, show schedules, dining reservations, and an interactive map to navigate the park efficiently.

Magic Guides: These offer tips, itineraries, and reviews from seasoned Disney travelers, helping you plan the perfect trip.

Transportation Apps: Use Google Maps and RATP apps to plan your travel to and from the park, especially if you're using public transportation.

Transportation Tips on How to Get to Disneyland Paris

1. By Air: Arriving in Paris

Main Airports: Charles de Gaulle Airport (CDG):

Distance: Coming from Disneyland Paris it is 43 km (27 miles)
Travel Time: 40 minutes by train or car to say approximately.

Options:

- **TGV Train**: Highspeed trains connect CDG to MarnelaVallée Chessy (Disneyland Paris station) in about 10 minutes.

- **Magic Shuttle Bus**: Operates directly between CDG and Disneyland hotels. Journey takes about 1 hour.

- **Taxi/Private Transfer**: Costs approximately €80–€100 and takes around 40–60 minutes.

2. Orly Airport (ORY):

Distance: Coming from Disneyland Paris 48 km (30 miles).

Travel Time: Approximately 50 minutes by train or car.

Options:

- **RER Train + TGV or RER A**: Take the Orlyval shuttle train to Antony, connect to the RER B, and then transfer to the RER A or TGV to MarnelaVallée Chessy.

- **Magic Shuttle Bus**: Journey time is about 1 hour.

- **Taxi/Private Transfer:** Costs approximately €90–€120 and takes around 50–70 minutes.

3. BeauvaisTillé Airport (BVA):

Disneyland Paris is 120 kilometers (75 miles) away.

Travel Time: Approximately 1.5–2 hours.

Options:

- **Bus to Paris + RER A Train**: Take the airport bus to Porte Maillot in Paris, then connect to RER A to MarnelaVallée Chessy.

- **Taxi/Private Transfer:** Costs approximately €150–€200 and takes 1.5–2 hours.

2. By Train: Convenient and Fast

High Speed Trains (TGV):

Direct Service: TGV trains from major cities in France (e.g., Lyon, Marseille) and neighboring countries (e.g., London via Eurostar, Brussels via Thalys) connect directly to MarnelaVallée Chessy station.

Travel Time: Paris to Disneyland Paris by TGV is just 10 minutes.

RER Regional Train (RER A Line):

From Central Paris:

Depart from major stations such as ChâteletLes Halles, Gare de Lyon, or Charles de Gaulle Étoile.

- Travel Time: Approximately 35–45 minutes.

- Frequency: Every 10–15 minutes.

- Ticket Price: Around €7.60 (oneway).

3. **By Car: Flexible and Convenient**

Driving Directions: From Paris, travel to Metz/Nancy via the A4 motorway (Autoroute de l'Est) and follow the Disneyland Paris signs. At MarnelaVallée, exit.

Parking: There are several parking options offered by Disneyland.

Standard Parking: €30 per day.

Hotel Parking: Included for guests staying at Disneyland hotels.

Travel Time: Approximately 40 minutes from central Paris, depending on traffic.

Tips:

- Always on and use your GPS or navigation app for real-time updates.

- Consider parking availability during peak seasons.

4. By Bus/Coach: Budget-Friendly Options

Shuttle Services:

1. Magic Shuttle:

- They often operates between Disneyland Paris and the airports (CDG, ORY) daily.

- Comfortable, family-friendly, and reliable.

2. Tourist Buses: Depart from key locations in Paris, such as the Eiffel Tower or Gare du Nord.

- Often included as part of Disneyland ticket packages.

3. **Public Bus Services**: Routes are limited and less convenient for tourists but are an option for budget travelers.

5. **By Taxi or RideShare**: Direct and HassleFree

Options:

Taxis: Widely available at airports, train stations, and throughout Paris.

- Ride Sharing Apps: Services like Uber and Bolt operate in Paris and its suburbs.

Estimated Costs:

- From Central Paris: €70–€90.

- From CDG Airport: €80–€100.

- From ORY Airport: €90–€120.

Travel Time: Approximately 40–60 minutes, depending on traffic.

6. For International Visitors: Special Services

Eurostar (London to Disneyland Paris):

Direct trains from London St Pancras International to MarnelaVallée Chessy.

Travel Time: 2 hours and 40 minutes to say approximately.

Frequency: Limited direct services; check schedules.

Thalys and TGV (Brussels, Amsterdam, and Beyond): Direct or connecting services to Disneyland Paris.

Travel Time: Varies by origin.

7. **Additional Tips for a Smooth Journey**

- Book in Advance: Especially for TGV, Eurostar, and shuttle services, as tickets can sell out quickly.

- Check Timetables: Train and shuttle schedules may vary based on the season or day of the week.

- Pack Essentials: Have tickets, passports (if traveling internationally), and a charged phone with navigation apps ready.

CHAPTER 3

DISNEYLAND PARK OVERVIEW

Main Street, U.S.A.

Fantasyland

Adventureland

Frontierland

Discoveryland

Walt Disney Studios Park

Overview and Themed Lands

Current Expansion Projects (Frozen Land and Lion King Land)

Park Overview

Disneyland Paris Theme Parks, Disneyland Park Paris, Main Street, U.S.A.

1. Main Street, U.S.A.

Longing for a glimpse of oldtime America? Take a stroll down Main Street, U.S.A., where you'll find classic brickpaved roads, vintage cars, and horsedrawn carriages capturing a bygone era.

Attractions: The Discovery Arcade celebrates 19thcentury innovations, while Liberty Arcade offers a captivating look at history and art from days past.

Entertainment: Enjoy the daily parade featuring beloved Disney characters and stay to watch the dazzling Disney Illuminations show.

Restaurants: Step into Walt's to experience the spirit of Walt Disney and his timeless creations.

Shops: Victorianthemed stores offer Disney souvenirs and memorabilia.

2. Frontierland

Transport yourself to a mini Wild West adventure in Frontierland, where your inner cowboy or cowgirl can shine.

Attractions: The eerie Phantom Manor will give you chills, and you can test your aim at the Rustler Roundup Shootin' Gallery.

Rides: Big Thunder Mountain and Thunder Mesa Riverboat Landing are iconic rides that can't be missed.

Entertainment: Watch The Lion King show and tour the Pocahontas Indian Village for a unique experience.

Restaurants: Indulge in juicy steaks at Silver Spur Steakhouse or Cowboy Cookout Barbecue.

3. Adventureland

Adventureland offers a haven for the daring, featuring seafaring escapades and pirate encounters.

Attractions: At La Cabane des Robinson, discover shipwreck survival skills and tropical wonder.

Rides: Indiana Jones and the Temple of Peril will thrill brave souls seeking adventure.

Entertainment: Board the Pirate Galleon with Captain Hook and embark on a quest for treasure.

Restaurants: Reenergize at Hakuna Matata or Captain Jack's for pirateworthy meals.

4. Fantasyland

A heartwarming land where fairy tales come to life, Fantasyland invites you to encounter cherished Disney characters and embrace magical stories.

Attractions: Sleeping Beauty's Castle is a mustsee landmark and sets the stage for the nightly Illuminations show.

Rides: Spin around in oversized teacups at Mad Hatter's Tea Cups and soar over London in Peter Pan's Flight.

Entertainment: Follow the White Rabbit's path through Alice's Curious Labyrinth.

Restaurants: Enjoy an intimate dinner at Pizzeria Bella Notte or meet Disney characters at Auberge de Cendrillon.

5. Discoveryland

Journey to the final frontier in Discoveryland, where the spacethemed landscape celebrates outer space exploration.

Attractions: Take the wheel in your own spaceship on Orbitron, a futuristic car ride.

Rides: Star Tours transports you to planet Endor, and Buzz Lightyear's Laser Blast lets you battle Emperor Zurg.

Entertainment: Face Darth Vader, a thrill for many Star Wars fans.

Restaurants: Buzz Lightyear's Pizza Planet Restaurant offers an allyoucaneat buffet to fuel your adventure.

Zones of Walt Disney Studios Park

Disneyland Paris Theme Parks, Walt Disney Studios Park, Marvel Avengers Campus

1. Marvel Avengers Campus

The newest addition, Marvel Avengers Campus, invites you to join heroes like Thor and Black Widow, even if only for a day.

Attractions: Stark Factory is a gathering place for superheroes to fix their gear.

Rides: Battle villains on Flight Force or join SpiderMan on his WEB Adventure to save the day.

Restaurants: PYM Kitchen showcases AntMan's power, where food sizes might surprise you.

2. Worlds of Pixar

Like Fantasyland, Worlds of Pixar brings beloved animated characters to life.

Attractions: Ride alongside Lightning McQueen at Cars Quatre Roues Rallye.

Rides: Board a turtle shell on Crush's Coaster and swim with Nemo through the Great Barrier Reef.

Entertainment: Step into Toy Story Playland to enjoy scenes and games inspired by Toy Story.

Restaurants: At Bistrot Chez Rémy, dine in a setting straight out of Ratatouille, complete with giant decor.

3. Front Lot

Modeled after Walt Disney's Hyperion Avenue Studios in Los Angeles, this zone is a tribute to Hollywood's golden age.

Attractions: Visit Disney Studio 1 to experience the film industry's glamorous early years.

Entertainment: Explore the Sorcerer's Apprentice fountain or see the famous Earful Tower landmark.

Restaurants: Dine at the iconic Restaurant en Coulisse.

Shops: Les Légendes d'Hollywood offers Disney merchandise and souvenirs.

4. Production Courtyard

Embrace the magic of cinema at the Production Courtyard.

Attractions: Help bring Disney Junior Dream Factory to life with song and dance.

Rides: Take a thrilling drop on the elevator at Hollywood Tower Hotel.

Entertainment: Watch Disney Junior Live On Stage and the Stitch Live! show.

Restaurants: Sample traditional French cuisine at Restaurant des Stars.

5. Toon Studio

Toon Studio is a paradise for animation enthusiasts and aspiring artists.

Attractions: Learn the craft of Disney and Pixar animation at Animation Studio.

Rides: Take flight on the Magic Carpets of Agrabah and soar through Arabian skies.

Entertainment: Enjoy Frozen the musical, starring Elsa, Anna, Olaf, and friends.

Highlights of Disneyland Paris

No matter your age or party size, there's something for everyone at Disneyland Paris. Here's what not to miss:

Character Dining: Have meals with Disney characters as they visit your table for unforgettable interactions.

Rides: Every zone offers fun rides for everyone to enjoy.

Shows and Musicals: Sing along with Frozen or watch a Lion King spectacle.

Accommodation: Extend the magic by staying at a Disneythemed hotel, where early access to the parks is a perk.

Festivals: Celebrate Christmas or Halloween at Disneyland Paris with seasonal festivities.

Themed Worlds: Traverse unique worlds, from African savannahs to retro American diners, each offering a new Disney adventure.

CHAPTER 4

TICKETING AND PASSES

Ticket Options and Prices

SingleDay Tickets

MultiDay Tickets

Annual Passes

Undated Tickets

Disney Premier Access and FastPass Options

Ticketing and Passes

Planning your visit to Disneyland Paris involves understanding the various ticket options available. Each type of ticket offers different benefits, depending on the length of your stay and the flexibility you need.

Ticket Options and Prices

SingleDay Tickets:

This type is ideal for visitors with limited time, singleday tickets grant access to one or both parks for one day. Prices vary based on the season, day of the week, and whether you choose to visit one park or both.

Price Range: Approximately €50 to €100 for adults and €45 to €90 for children.

MultiDay Tickets:

These tickets are perfect for those who want to explore the parks more leisurely over several days. Multiday tickets provide access to both Disneyland Park and Walt Disney Studios Park.

Price Range: The cost per day decreases with the number of days purchased. For example, a threeday adult ticket may cost around €180, while a fiveday ticket might be €250.

Annual Passes:

Annual passes offer unlimited access to the parks throughout the year, along with a variety of perks like discounts on dining, shopping, and hotel stays. There are several types of annual passes, each with different levels of access and benefits.

Types of Passes:

Discovery Pass: Basic pass with some blackout dates.

Magic Flex Pass: Fewer blackout dates and additional discounts.

Magic Plus Pass: Minimal blackout dates, with more discounts and perks.

Infinity Pass: Premium pass with no blackout dates and maximum benefits.

Price Range: Annual passes range from approximately €179 for the Discovery Pass to €499 for the Infinity Pass.

Undated Tickets:

These tickets provide the flexibility to visit the parks on any date, making them a great option for those who want to keep their plans open.

Price Range: Typically more expensive than dated tickets, but they offer the convenience of not having to commit to a specific date.

Disney Premier Access and FastPass Options

Disney Premier Access:

This paid service allows you to skip the regular lines for some of the most popular attractions by booking a specific time slot to ride. You can purchase Premier Access for individual attractions or as a bundle.

How It Works: Use the official Disneyland Paris app to select your desired attraction and time slot. Prices vary depending on the attraction and demand.

Benefits: Great for maximizing your time in the parks, especially on busy days.

FastPass:

Disneyland Paris previously offered the FastPass system, allowing guests to reserve access to shorter lines for popular attractions at no extra cost. However, this system has been replaced by the paid Disney Premier Access service.

Tips: Keep an eye on announcements for any changes or updates to the FastPass system, as Disneyland Paris continually evolves its offerings.

Understanding these ticket options and services will help you make the most of your visit to Disneyland Paris, ensuring you have the flexibility and access you need to enjoy the parks fully.

CHAPTER 5

ACCOMMODATIONS

Disneyland Hotel (Luxury Option)

The Disney Hotel New York

Disney Newport Bay Club

Disney Sequoia Lodge

Disney Hotel Cheyenne

Disney Hotel Santa Fe

Disney Davy Crockett Ranch

Booking Tips and Package Options

Accommodations

Choosing the right place to stay is crucial for making the most of your Disneyland Paris experience. The resort offers a range of hotels to suit different budgets and preferences, each with its own unique theme and benefits.

Disneyland Paris boasts a variety of hotels, each designed to provide guests with an immersive Disney experience while ensuring comfort and convenience. Staying at a Disney hotel offers several perks, including early park entry, free shuttle service to the parks, and themed decor that extends the magic of your visit.

Disneyland Hotel (Luxury Option)

This is the toptier option for guests looking for luxury and elegance. The Disneyland Hotel is located right at the entrance of Disneyland Park, making it the most convenient choice. Styled in Victorian elegance, it feels grand and regal, like stepping back in time to a luxurious palace. The rooms are spacious, with highquality furnishings, and some even have views of the park itself. Guests here can enjoy fine dining, a relaxing spa, and exclusive character experiences that make for special memories.

Theme: Victorianstyle luxury with a touch of Disney elegance.

Location: Situated at the entrance of Disneyland Park, offering the closest access to the park.

Amenities: Features include fine dining restaurants, a luxurious spa, an indoor swimming pool, and exclusive character meetandgreets.

Highlights:

VIP Services: Enjoy personalized services such as private checkin and concierge assistance.

Views: Many rooms offer stunning views of the park, allowing you to watch the nighttime fireworks from the comfort of your room.

The Disney Hotel New York

Fans of Marvel superheroes, this hotel brings your favorite characters to life with art and decor inspired by Marvel's universe. Disney Hotel New York – The Art of Marvel is designed to look like a sleek New York City skyscraper and features over 350 pieces of Marvel artwork, including unique displays and sculptures. The rooms have a modern city feel with superherothemed art. There's also a Marvel Hero Training Zone where kids can enjoy an Avengersstyle workout. This hotel combines style, fun, and adventure for Marvel fans and families alike.

Theme: Combines the elegance of New York City with the excitement of Marvel superheroes.

Location: A short walk from Disney Village and the theme parks.

Amenities: Features include themed suites, a Marvel art gallery, a rooftop bar, and a pool.

Highlights:

Marvel Experience: Offers unique experiences such as superhero training sessions and opportunities to meet your favorite Marvel characters.

Art and Design: The hotel showcases original Marvel artwork, making it a mustvisit for fans of the franchise.

Disney Newport Bay Club

This seasideinspired hotel gives you a calm, coastal feel, perfect for relaxing after a day at the parks. Disney Newport Bay Club resembles a grand, oldfashioned yacht club, with blue and white decor that makes you feel like you're on a New England vacation. Located along Lake Disney, this hotel offers beautiful waterfront views and a peaceful atmosphere. The rooms are nautically themed, and there's a large indoor and outdoor pool area. It's a midrange option, ideal for families wanting a balanced mix of comfort and price.

Theme: Nautical New England style, reminiscent of a 1920s coastal resort.

Location: Overlooks Lake Disney, about a 15minute walk from the parks.

Amenities: Features include two swimming pools, a fitness center, and character dining options.

Highlights:

Lakeside Charm: Enjoy picturesque views of Lake Disney and elegant decor that transports you to a seaside retreat.

FamilyFriendly: Offers spacious family rooms and a variety of activities for children.

Disney Sequoia Lodge

Disney Sequoia Lodge is designed for nature lovers. Inspired by America's national parks, it has a rustic, lodgelike style with warm, earthy tones and wooden decor. Surrounded by pine trees, this hotel feels cozy and natural, perfect for unwinding. The rooms are themed around Bambi and other woodland creatures, and the indoor pool area even features a slide designed to look like a tree trunk. It's a midrange choice with a relaxed vibe, offering a unique contrast to the lively theme parks.

Theme: Inspired by American national parks, featuring rustic wood and stone decor.

Location: Located on the shores of Lake Disney, about a 15minute walk from the parks.

Amenities: Includes an indoor swimming pool with a slide, a fitness center, and cozy fireplaces.

Highlights:

Nature Vibes: The lodge's design and surroundings create a tranquil, forestlike atmosphere.

Comfort: Offers comfortable rooms and suites, perfect for families and nature lovers.

Disney Hotel Cheyenne

Step into the Wild West at Disney Hotel Cheyenne. This hotel is designed like an old western town, complete with saloons, sheriff offices, and cowboythemed rooms. Disney Hotel Cheyenne is one of the more budgetfriendly options but still provides fun, themed details that make it feel immersive. The rooms feature Woody from Toy Story, making it a hit with kids. It's located a bit farther from the parks but offers shuttle services, making it a convenient yet affordable choice for families.

Theme: Westernthemed, designed to resemble a frontier town from the Wild West.

Location: Approximately a 20minute walk from the parks, with shuttle service available.

Amenities: Features include bunk beds for kids, a saloonthemed restaurant, and an outdoor play area.

Highlights:

Themed Rooms: Rooms are decorated with Toy Story's Woody and other Western motifs, making it fun for kids.

Western Experience: The hotel's design and atmosphere transport you to a classic Wild West setting.

Disney Hotel Santa Fe

Inspired by the landscapes of the American Southwest, Disney Hotel Santa Fe has a relaxed, desertthemed atmosphere. Decorated with warm, earthy colors and designs inspired by Native American culture, this hotel provides a unique experience for those looking for budgetfriendly accommodations. The rooms feature the characters from Cars, making it especially popular with younger children. Like Hotel Cheyenne, it's a bit farther from the parks but has convenient shuttle services. This hotel is ideal for guests wanting a different style at a lower price.

Theme: Inspired by the American Southwest and the DisneyPixar film Cars.

Location: About a 20minute walk from the parks, with shuttle service available.

Amenities: Includes a themed restaurant, a bar, and outdoor play areas.

Highlights:

CarsThemed Decor: Rooms feature Carsthemed decorations, perfect for young fans of the movie.

BudgetFriendly: Offers an affordable option without sacrificing the Disney magic.

Disney Davy Crockett Ranch

For those who prefer a more private and rustic experience, Disney Davy Crockett Ranch is a unique option. Located about a 15minute drive from the parks, it offers private cabins in a peaceful, wooded area. Each cabin includes a kitchen, making it a good choice for families or groups who want to selfcater. There's a variety of outdoor activities available, such as a swimming pool, tree climbing, and minigolf. This hotel doesn't have direct park shuttles, so you'll need a car, but it's a fantastic choice for nature lovers looking for a peaceful retreat.

Theme: A rustic, cabinstyle resort located in a wooded area.

Location: About a 15minute drive from the parks, with parking available (no shuttle service).

Amenities: Features include an indoor pool, a fitness trail, and outdoor sports facilities.

Highlights:

SelfCatering Cabins: Each cabin has a kitchenette and outdoor BBQ area, ideal for families or groups.

Nature Retreat: Offers a more secluded, natureoriented experience away from the hustle and bustle of the parks.

Booking Tips and Package Options
Booking Tips:

- When booking a Disneyland Paris hotel, consider purchasing a package that includes park tickets. This often saves money compared to booking them separately. Disney frequently offers seasonal deals, such as discounts on hotel rates or extra days in the parks, so keep an eye out for promotions, especially if you book in advance.

- Consider the benefits of staying at a Disney hotel, like early park entry and character experiences, which can make your trip even more magical. If you plan to visit during busy times, booking early helps secure your spot. For larger groups, Disney Davy Crockett Ranch is ideal due to its spacious cabins, while families with young children might prefer Disney Hotel New York for its superhero experience or the Disneyland Hotel for its prime location.

- Whether you're looking for luxury, comfort

- **Plan Early**: Popular hotels can book up quickly, especially during peak seasons. Book as early as possible.
- **Look for Deals**: Check for special offers and packages, such as seasonal discounts or bundled park tickets and meals.

- **Consider Packages:** Disneyland Paris often offers packages that include hotel stays, park tickets, and dining plans, which can provide significant savings.

Package Options:

Hotel and Ticket Packages: Combine your hotel stay with park tickets for a convenient allinone solution.

Meal Plans: Add meal plans to your package to enjoy hasslefree dining options throughout your stay.

Choosing the right accommodation can enhance your Disneyland Paris experience, providing comfort, convenience, and a touch of Disney magic throughout your visit.

Things to Know for a Smooth Disneyland Paris Hotel Stay

Staying at a Disneyland Paris hotel is a fantastic choice, not only for its convenience to the parks but also for the unique experience it offers. Here are some helpful tips if you're planning to stay at a Disney hotel.

Before Booking

When booking, you'll need to fill out a personal information form. Afterward, reserve a table for lunch or dinner at one of the hotel's restaurants. Make sure to download the Disneyland Paris app, which has show schedules, recommendations, and other essential information for your visit. Be sure to review the health and safety guidelines provided by the hotel for a safe stay.

Upon Arrival

Check in at the hotel at or after 10 AM, where you can pick up your Park tickets and any documents needed for your stay. You'll also receive your allinone MagicPass, which grants you access to your room, meal vouchers, park tickets, and amenities like the fitness centers and pools. You can leave your luggage in the Luggage Room and head straight to the parks via shuttle, by foot, or by car. Take time during your stay to explore the exclusive activities the hotel has for guests.

CheckOut

You'll need to check out by 11 AM, at which point your key card will deactivate. Any pending charges will be settled automatically, and your account with the hotel will be closed. You're welcome to leave your bags in the luggage room or your car while enjoying the park a bit longer before heading out.

Hotel Policies at Disneyland Paris

If you're staying at a Disneyland Paris hotel, here are some guidelines to be aware of:

- Security checks may be conducted at entrances and within the hotels. Refusal of inspection can result in being denied entry.
- Alcohol, illegal substances, glass containers, hazardous items, and toy weapons (like laser guns or water pistols) are prohibited.
- Loud objects like megaphones or horns are not allowed.
- Remotecontrolled devices, including drones, are restricted.

- Roller skates, bicycles, and scooters cannot be used inside the hotels, though they may be permitted outdoors at Disney Davy Crockett Ranch.
- Guests must follow the dress codes set by hotel restaurants, and headwear covering the face is restricted for visitors over 12, except for medical reasons.
- Minors (under 18) cannot stay without supervision.
- Only assistance animals are allowed, and they must be leashed.
- Alcohol may only be consumed if purchased at hotel bars or restaurants.
- All indoor areas, including rooms and covered outdoor spaces, are nonsmoking zones.
- Photos and videos are allowed only for personal use.
- Standard checkin is 3 PM and checkout is 11 AM, except at Disney Davy Crockett Ranch, where checkin is at 4 PM.

Nearby Hotels to Disneyland Paris

If you're unable to secure a room at a Disneyland hotel or prefer another option, here are some nearby accommodations:

Luxury Options

1. Adagio MarnelaVallee Val d'Europe
   - Price per night for 2: $380 $950

- **Amenities**: Free parking, WiFi, inhouse dining and bars, luggage service, access to both parks, extra magic time, room service, toiletries, air conditioning, indoor pool, accessible features, and more.

Dining Options for Nearby Hotels

Luxury

Adagio MarnelaVallee Val d'Europe

Dining Options:

- **Breakfast Room**: Start your day with a hearty continental breakfast buffet in the cozy breakfast room.

- **Apartment Kitchen**: Enjoy the convenience of a fully equipped kitchen in your apartment to prepare your own meals.

MidRange

B&B Hotel

Dining Options:

- **Breakfast Room**: Indulge in a gourmet breakfast with a selection of sweet and savory options before heading to the parks.

- **Les Halles**: Enjoy pizzas, pasta, salads, and more with a scenic lake view.

- **BAR**: Unwind with a variety of drinks after a day of adventure.

Hotel l'Elysee Val d'Europe

Dining Options:

- **Le George**: Delight in fine cuts of meat and organic, glutenfree options crafted from fresh ingredients.
- **Le Diplomate**: Relax with a drink and delicious food at this inviting bar.

Radisson Blu Hotel Marne La Vallee

Dining Options:

Le Pamplemousse: Savor modern and classic dishes paired with wines and spirits, with a view of the golf course.

Le Birdie: Enjoy a robust breakfast featuring hot and cold options.

Le Chardon: Relax by the fireplace with cocktails and signature drinks.

Budget

Campanile Val de France

Dining Options:

- **Le Marche Gourmand**: Enjoy a continental breakfast buffet or traditional French meals.
- **Sushi Bar:** Dive into expertly crafted sushi, makis, and sashimi.
- **House Burger**: Treat yourself to homemade burgers and fries.
- **Le Bar**: Open 24/7, offering sandwiches, salads, paninis, and pasta.

Dream Castle Fabulous Hotels Group

Dining Options:

- **The Bosquet Gourmand Restaurant**: This buffet restaurant serves cold cuts, pastries, scrambled eggs, and fruit juices, plus a Kids' Corner with treats for children.

- **Astrolabe Bar:** Enjoy cocktails and bites like burgers and salads under zodiacinspired decor.

Explorers Fabulous Hotels Group

Dining Options:

- Buffet Restaurant La Plantation: A breakfast spread inspired by global flavors.

- **Marco's Pizza Parlor**: Quick pizzas, fries, salads, and desserts.

- **Captain's Library Restaurant**: Savor gourmet French cuisine in a cozy atmosphere.

- **The Candy's Tavern**: Enjoy sweet treats, caramel, and refreshing liquors.

- **Trader's Bar:** Relax with wine, cocktails, and finger foods after a day of fun.

- **Snack Bar Point Gourmand**: Enjoy sweet and savory snacks with refreshing drinks.

Magic Circus Fabulous Hotels Group

Dining Options:

- La Table de Monsieur Maurice: Indulge in balanced, gourmet dishes in a vibrant, friendly atmosphere.
- **Chez Maurice**: Feast on international dishes with garden views from the terrace.
- **Magic'Hall Bar**: Unwind with a drink after a day in the parks.

Budget summary for the hotels at Disneyland Paris

HOTEL	TYPE	PRICE PER NIGHT	DISTANCE TO PARK	SPECIAL FEATURES
Disneyland Hotel	Luxury	€350 €600	Entrance	Victorianstyle luxury, fine dining, spa, character meetandgreets
Disney Hotel New York – The Art of Marvel	Moderate	€200 €400	10minute walk	Marvelthemed, rooftop bar, Marvel art gallery
Disney Newport Bay Club	Moderate	€150 €350	15minute walk	Nautical New England style, two swimming pools, fitness center
Disney Sequoia Lodge	Moderate	€150 €350	15minute walk	Rustic lodge, indoor pool with slide, fitness trail
Disney Hotel Cheyenne	Moderate	€150 €350	20minute walk	Westernthemed, bunk beds for kids,

				saloonthemed restaurant
Disney Hotel Santa Fe	Budget	€100 €300	20minute walk	Carsthemed, outdoor play areas, budgetfriendly
Disney Davy Crockett Ranch	Budget	€100 €300	15minute drive	Selfcatering cabins, outdoor BBQ area, nature retreat

CHAPTER 6

ATTRACTIONS AND RIDES

Overview of Popular Attractions

Classic Rides

- "It's a Small World"
- "Pirates of the Caribbean"
- "Big Thunder Mountain"

Thrill Rides

- "Hyperspace Mountain"
- "Indiana Jones and the Temple of Peril"

FamilyFriendly Attractions

- "Peter Pan's Flight"
- "Ratatouille: The Adventure"

Attractions and Rides

Disneyland Paris is renowned for its wide range of attractions and rides that cater to all ages and preferences. From classic Disney rides to thrilling roller coasters and immersive familyfriendly experiences, there is something for everyone to enjoy. Here's a detailed look at some of the standout attractions in both Disneyland Park and Walt Disney Studios Park:

Overview of Popular Attractions

Disneyland Paris features iconic attractions that have delighted visitors for years. These rides and experiences are a mustvisit for any trip to the park, offering a blend of nostalgia, adventure, and magic that only Disney can provide.

Classic Rides

"It's a Small World":

- **Location:** Fantasyland, Disneyland Park
- **Description:** This beloved ride takes visitors on a gentle boat journey through scenes representing different cultures from around the world, accompanied by the iconic song "It's a Small World."
- **Highlights:** The vibrant scenes, cheerful music, and intricate details make it a favorite for all ages. It's a celebration of global unity and peace, wrapped in the whimsical charm of Disney.

"Pirates of the Caribbean":

- **Location:** Adventureland, Disneyland Park

- **Description:** Set sail on this classic dark ride that takes you through the world of pirates, with detailed animatronics, thrilling drops, and iconic scenes.
- **Highlights:** The elaborate sets, catchy theme song, and appearances by Captain Jack Sparrow create an unforgettable experience. The ride's mix of excitement and storytelling makes it a perennial favorite.

"Big Thunder Mountain":

- **Location:** Frontierland, Disneyland Park
- **Description:** This runaway mine train ride offers thrilling twists and turns through the wild west. It's one of the park's most popular attractions.
- **Highlights:** The ride's immersive theming, exciting drops, and beautiful scenery make it a mustdo. The story of the cursed mining town adds an extra layer of fun.

Thrill Rides

"Hyperspace Mountain":

- **Location:** Discoveryland, Disneyland Park
- **Description:** This highspeed roller coaster is themed around the Star Wars universe, taking riders on an exhilarating journey through space battles and missions.

- **Highlights:** The combination of thrilling loops, highspeed twists, and Star Wars theming creates an adrenalinepumping experience. The ride's soundtrack and special effects enhance the excitement.

"Indiana Jones and the Temple of Peril":

- **Location:** Adventureland, Disneyland Park
- **Description:** Join Indiana Jones on this adventurous roller coaster that features sharp turns, steep drops, and a thrilling loop.
- **Highlights:** The detailed queue area, inspired by the Indiana Jones movies, sets the stage for the adventure. The ride's fastpaced action and theming make it a hit for thrillseekers.

FamilyFriendly Attractions

"Peter Pan's Flight":

- **Location:** Fantasyland, Disneyland Park
- **Description:** Soar over London and Neverland on this gentle, suspended dark ride that follows the story of Peter Pan.
- **Highlights:** The charming scenes, smooth ride experience, and magical journey through the skies make it a favorite for families and children. The ride's unique perspective and storytelling bring the classic tale to life.

"Ratatouille: The Adventure":

- **Location:** Walt Disney Studios Park
- **Description:** This 4D dark ride shrinks visitors down to the size of a rat and takes them on a chaotic journey through Gusteau's restaurant, inspired by the Pixar film "Ratatouille."
- **Highlights:** The innovative ride technology, detailed sets, and immersive experience make it a standout attraction. The combination of 3D visuals, physical effects, and charming storyline creates a delightful adventure for all ages.

Disneyland Paris offers a diverse array of attractions that provide fun and excitement for everyone. Whether you're a fan of classic rides, thrill rides, or familyfriendly adventures, there's something to make your visit unforgettable.

CHAPTER 7

DINING EXPERIENCES

Character Dining Experiences

Themed Restaurants

- Auberge de Cendrillon
- Bistrot Chez Rémy
- Captain Jack's – Restaurant des Pirates

QuickService Options

Dining Reservations and Tips

Dining Experiences

Disneyland Paris offers a variety of dining experiences to suit every palate and preference. From character meals to themed restaurants, there's something to delight every visitor. Here's a detailed guide to help you plan your meals at the resort:

Character Dining Experiences

Overview: Character dining is a highlight at Disneyland Paris, offering guests the chance to enjoy a meal while interacting with their favorite Disney characters. These experiences are especially popular with families, as they provide memorable moments and great photo opportunities.

Options:

- **Auberge de Cendrillon:** Located in Fantasyland, this elegant restaurant offers a royal dining experience where guests can meet Disney Princesses such as Cinderella, Belle, and Aurora. The menu features fine French cuisine, including appetizers, main courses, and desserts.
- **Inventions:** Situated inside the Disneyland Hotel, Inventions offers a buffetstyle dining experience with a wide variety of dishes. Characters like Mickey, Minnie, and Goofy visit the tables, making it a fun and interactive meal for all ages.

Themed Restaurants

Disneyland Paris is home to several themed restaurants that provide unique dining experiences, transporting guests to different worlds and times through detailed decor and imaginative menus.

Auberge de Cendrillon:

- **Location:** Fantasyland, Disneyland Park
- **Theme:** Cinderella's fairy tale castle
- **Cuisine:** French fine dining
- **Highlights:** Dine in a royal setting with Disney Princesses. The menu features gourmet dishes such as filet mignon,

roasted duck, and delightful pastries. The enchanting atmosphere and character interactions make it a magical experience for everyone.

Bistrot Chez Rémy:

- **Location:** Walt Disney Studios Park
- **Theme:** Inspired by the movie Ratatouille
- **Cuisine:** French bistrostyle dishes
- **Highlights:** This unique restaurant shrinks guests down to the size of a rat, with oversized decor that recreates Rémy's world. The menu includes classic French dishes like ratatouille, steak, and a selection of fine cheeses. The whimsical setting and attention to detail make it a mustvisit.

Captain Jack's – Restaurant des Pirates:

- **Location:** Adventureland, Disneyland Park
- **Theme:** Pirate hideout
- **Cuisine:** Caribbeaninspired
- **Highlights:** Set within the Pirates of the Caribbean ride, this restaurant offers a swashbuckling dining experience. The menu features Caribbean dishes such as marinated shrimp, jerk chicken, and tropical fruit desserts. The dimly lit, piratethemed decor enhances the adventurous atmosphere.

QuickService Options

For those looking to grab a quick bite and get back to the action, Disneyland Paris offers numerous quickservice options that provide a variety of tasty meals and snacks:

- **Casey's Corner:** Located on Main Street, U.S.A., this Americanstyle eatery offers classic hot dogs, fries, and refreshing beverages.
- **Hakuna Matata:** Found in Adventureland, this restaurant serves Africaninspired dishes like kebabs, rice, and salads in a vibrant setting.
- **Pizzeria Bella Notte:** Situated in Fantasyland, this charming spot offers Italian favorites such as pizzas, pastas, and salads, inspired by Lady and the Tramp.

Dining Reservations and Tips

Reservations:

- **Why Reserve:** Dining reservations are highly recommended, especially for character meals and popular themed restaurants, as they tend to fill up quickly.
- **How to Reserve:** Reservations can be made up to 60 days in advance via the official Disneyland Paris app, website, or by calling the dining reservation line.
- **Tips:** If your preferred restaurant is fully booked, keep checking for cancellations or try to secure a reservation upon arrival at the park.

General Tips:

- **Plan Ahead:** Review restaurant menus and decide where you want to eat before your visit to ensure you enjoy the best dining experiences.
- **Timing:** Try to dine at offpeak hours (before noon or after 2 PM) to avoid long lines and crowded restaurants.
- **Special Dietary Needs:** Disneyland Paris accommodates various dietary needs, including vegetarian, vegan, glutenfree, and allergyfriendly options. Inform your server of any dietary restrictions, and they will assist you in selecting suitable menu items.

By exploring the diverse dining options at Disneyland Paris, you can enjoy a range of delicious meals while creating unforgettable memories with family and friends.

Budget summary of meals at Disneyland

RESTUARANT	TYPE	PRICE RANGE	LOCATION	SPECIAL FEATURES
Auberge de Cendrillon	Character Dining	€40 €75	Fantasyland, Disneyland Park	French fine dining, Disney Princesses
Bistrot Chez Rémy	Themed Restaurant	€30 €75	Walt Disney Studios Park	French bistrostyle, Ratatouille theme
Captain Jack's – Restaurant des Pirates	Themed Restaurant	€30 €75	Adventureland, Disneyland Park	Caribbeaninspired cuisine, Pirates of the Caribbean theme

Casey's Corner	Quick Service	€5 €10	Main Street, U.S.A., Disneyland Park	Americansty le hot dogs, fries, beverages
Pizzeria Bella Notte	Quick Service	€5 €10	Fantasyland, Disneyland Park	Italian favorites like pizzas, pastas, salads
Hakuna Matata	Quick Service	€5 €10	Adventurela nd, Disneyland Park	Africaninspired dishes like kebabs, rice, salads
Cable Car Bake Shop	Quick Service	€5 €10	Main Street, U.S.A.,	Americanstyle baked goods,

			Disneyland Park	pastries, beverages
Fantasia Gelati	Quick Service	€5 €10	Discoveryland, Disneyland ParkItalianstyle gelato, ice cream,	Italianstyle gelato, ice cream, desserts
The Gibson Girl Ice Cream Parlour	Quick Service	€5 €10	Main Street, U.S.A., Disneyland Park	Ice cream, sundaes, milkshakes

Dear firsttime travelers, please note that these prices are approximate and can vary based on the menu items selected, season, and any special promotions. It's always a good idea to check the official Disneyland Paris website or contact their dining services for the most uptodate information.

CHAPTER 8

ENTERTAINMENT AND SHOWS

- Parades and Seasonal Celebrations
- Character MeetandGreets
- Nighttime Spectaculars
- Upcoming Shows and New Attractions

Entertainment and Shows

Disneyland Paris offers a wealth of entertainment options beyond its rides and attractions. From dazzling parades to intimate character meetandgreets and stunning nighttime spectaculars, the resort provides countless ways to enjoy the magic of Disney. Here's a comprehensive guide to the entertainment and shows you can expect to find:

Parades and Seasonal Celebrations

Parades:

- **Disney Stars on Parade:** This lively daytime parade features colorful floats, beloved Disney characters, and catchy music. It's a mustsee event where you can wave to Mickey, Minnie, and their friends as they travel down Main Street, U.S.A.

- **Magic Happens Parade (Seasonal):** On special occasions and during certain seasons, Disneyland Paris hosts the Magic Happens Parade, showcasing an array of Disney stories with intricate floats and festive costumes.

Seasonal Celebrations:

- **Halloween Celebrations:** During October, the park transforms with spooky decorations, special shows, and character encounters featuring your favorite villains. Don't miss the Halloween Soirée, a special nighttime event with unique entertainment.
- **Disney Christmas Magic:** From November to January, the park sparkles with festive lights, a towering Christmas tree, and holidaythemed parades and shows. Santa Claus makes special appearances, adding to the holiday cheer.
- **Spring and Summer Events:** Throughout the warmer months, Disneyland Paris hosts a variety of events, including the Princess Run in spring and music festivals in summer, providing extra fun and entertainment for visitors.

Character MeetandGreets

Meeting Disney characters is a highlight for many visitors, and Disneyland Paris offers numerous opportunities for these magical encounters:

- **Meet Mickey Mouse:** Visit Mickey in his specially designed house in Fantasyland, where you can take photos and get autographs.
- **Princess Pavilion:** Meet Disney Princesses in this elegant setting in Fantasyland. Each visit provides a personal moment with a beloved princess.
- **Marvel Superheroes:** At Disney Hotel New York – The Art of Marvel, guests can meet Marvel superheroes such as SpiderMan, Iron Man, and Captain America.

Nighttime Spectaculars

As the day draws to a close, Disneyland Paris comes alive with breathtaking nighttime shows:

- **Disney Illuminations:** This spectacular show at Sleeping Beauty Castle combines fireworks, projections, and music to create a mesmerizing experience. Scenes from classic Disney movies and new favorites are brought to life in a dazzling display.
- **Disney Dreams!:** Another stunning nighttime show that features projections onto Sleeping Beauty Castle, accompanied by fireworks and fountains. The show's storytelling and visual effects make it a mustsee.
- **Star Wars: A Galactic Celebration (Seasonal):** On selected nights, Walt Disney Studios Park hosts this special event,

where iconic Star Wars scenes are projected onto the Tower of Terror, along with lasers, fireworks, and music from the saga.

Upcoming Shows and New Attractions

Disneyland Paris continually updates its entertainment offerings, ensuring there's always something new to experience:

- **Frozen Celebration:** A new show featuring characters and songs from Disney's Frozen, set to debut in the upcoming year. Expect dazzling effects and heartwarming performances.
- **Lion King and Jungle Festival:** This summer festival includes stage shows, parades, and interactive experiences inspired by The Lion King and The Jungle Book. It's a vibrant celebration of music and storytelling.

Disneyland Paris offers a diverse array of entertainment and shows that enhance the magic of your visit. Be sure to check the daily schedule for showtimes and plan your day to include these memorable experiences.

CHAPTER 9

SHOPPING AND SOUVENIRS

- Main Street Shopping Highlights
- Unique Disneyland Paris Merchandise
- Special Souvenirs and Gift Ideas

Shopping and Souvenirs

Disneyland Paris offers a fantastic array of shopping opportunities, allowing you to take a piece of the magic home with you. From themed merchandise to unique souvenirs, there's something for everyone to cherish as a memory of their visit. Here's a detailed guide to the best shopping spots and what you can find:

Main Street Shopping Highlights

Main Street, U.S.A.:

- **Emporium:** The largest store in Disneyland Paris, the Emporium offers a wide variety of Disney merchandise, including clothing, toys, home decor, and souvenirs. It's a great place to start your shopping adventure.
- **Disney Clothiers, Ltd.:** This shop specializes in Disneythemed clothing and accessories for all ages. You'll find everything from stylish apparel to cozy pajamas.

- **Boardwalk Candy Palace:** A sweettooth haven, this store features a range of delicious treats, including candies, chocolates, and freshly made pastries. It's also a great place to find themed holiday treats during special seasons.
- **The Storybook Store:** Focused on books and media, this shop offers a selection of Disneythemed literature, including storybooks, coloring books, and DVDs.

Unique Disneyland Paris Merchandise

Disneyland Paris has exclusive merchandise that you won't find at other Disney parks. Here are some unique items to look out for:

- **Limited Edition Pins:** Collectible pins featuring unique designs, characters, and special events. Pin trading is also a popular activity among guests.
- **Disneyland Paris Apparel:** Exclusive clothing items that celebrate the park, including Tshirts, hoodies, and hats featuring the park's logo and beloved characters.
- **FrenchInspired Items:** Merchandise that blends Disney magic with French culture, such as Minnie Mouse in a beret or Mickeythemed Eiffel Tower souvenirs.

- **AttractionSpecific Items:** Souvenirs themed to specific rides and attractions, like Hyperspace Mountain shirts or Phantom Manor collectibles.

Special Souvenirs and Gift Ideas

Whether you're looking for the perfect gift or a special keepsake, Disneyland Paris offers a variety of unique and memorable items:

- **Personalized Merchandise:** Some shops offer personalized items, such as engraved glassware, customized ear hats, and embroidered clothing.
- **Art and Collectibles:** The Art of Disney on Main Street, U.S.A. features a selection of fine art, limited edition prints, and collectibles. It's the perfect place to find a special piece to commemorate your visit.
- **Jewelry and Accessories:** Shops like L'Atelier de la Reine and Arribas France offer beautiful jewelry and accessories, including Swarovski crystal pieces and Disneythemed charms.
- **Home Decor:** Bring a touch of Disney magic to your home with decorative items like picture frames, kitchenware, and holiday ornaments.

Shopping at Disneyland Paris is an adventure in itself, offering a wide range of items that capture the magic and joy of the park. Be sure to set aside time to explore the many stores and find the perfect souvenirs to remember your visit.

An estimated budget for shopping at Disneyland Paris

ITEMS	ESTIMATED COST (per person)	NOTES
Small Souvenirs (pins, keychains)	€15 €30	Collectible pins and keychains are popular choices.
Clothing (Tshirts, hoodies)	€30 €100	Disneythemed apparel, including shirts, hoodies, and hats.
Plush Toys	€20 €50	Soft toys featuring favorite Disney characters.
Jewelry and Accessories	€50 €100	Items like bracelets, necklaces, and watches with Disney themes.

Home Decor (picture frames, ornaments)	€20 €50	Decorative items to bring a touch of Disney magic home.
Art and Collectibles	€50 €100	Limited edition prints, fine art, and collectibles.
Photopass	€60 €70	For capturing ride photos and character encounters.
Games and Activities	€10 €20	Arcade games and other activities not included in the park ticket.
Miscellaneous (snacks, drinks)	€10 €20	Extra budget for snacks, drinks, and unexpected expenses.

CHAPTER 10

SEASONAL EVENTS AND FESTIVITIES

- Halloween Celebrations
- Disney Christmas Magic
- Spring and Summer Events
- 100th Disney Anniversary Celebrations

Seasonal Events and Festivities

Disneyland Paris hosts a variety of seasonal events and festivities throughout the year, each adding a unique touch of magic to the park. These events often include special decorations, themed entertainment, exclusive merchandise, and seasonal food and beverages. Here's a detailed guide to the main seasonal events at Disneyland Paris:

Halloween Celebrations

Overview: During the Halloween season, Disneyland Paris transforms into a spooky wonderland. The parks are adorned with festive decorations, including pumpkins, ghosts, and autumnal colors. This celebration typically runs from early October to early November.

Highlights:

- **Disney Villains:** Meet some of your favorite Disney villains, such as Maleficent, Ursula, and Captain Hook, who make special appearances during this time.
- **Mickey's Halloween Celebration:** Enjoy a festive parade featuring Mickey and friends dressed in their Halloween costumes, along with themed floats and music.
- **Halloween Soirée:** On select nights, the park hosts a special ticketed event with exclusive entertainment, character meetandgreets, and extended park hours.

Disney Christmas Magic

Overview: From midNovember to early January, Disneyland Paris becomes a winter wonderland, celebrating the holiday season with stunning decorations, festive entertainment, and a magical atmosphere.

Highlights:

- **Christmas Decorations:** The parks and hotels are beautifully decorated with twinkling lights, Christmas trees, and seasonal displays. Main Street, U.S.A., in particular, is a sight to behold.

- **Christmas Parade:** Watch the Disney's Christmas Parade, featuring beloved characters in festive attire, themed floats, and cheerful music.
- **Santa Claus:** Meet Santa Claus and take part in special holidaythemed meetandgreets with other characters dressed in their winter outfits.
- **Christmas Tree Lighting Ceremony:** Enjoy the nightly ceremony where Mickey and friends light up the grand Christmas tree on Main Street, U.S.A.

Spring and Summer Events

Spring:

- **Swing into Spring:** This event celebrates the arrival of spring with beautiful floral displays, lively entertainment, and special activities. Disney characters don their springtime attire, and the park is filled with vibrant colors and decorations.

Summer:

- **Marvel Super Heroes Season:** Join the Marvel superheroes for a summer of actionpacked fun at Walt Disney Studios Park. Enjoy shows, meetandgreets, and special events featuring characters like SpiderMan, Iron Man, and Captain America.
- **Electroland:** This summer music festival brings DJs and electronic dance music to Walt Disney Studios Park,

combining thrilling rides with live performances and dazzling light shows.

100th Disney Anniversary Celebrations

Overview: In honor of Disney's 100th anniversary, Disneyland Paris will host special events and celebrations throughout the year. This once in a lifetime celebration will feature exclusive entertainment, unique merchandise, and festive decorations.

Highlights:

- **Centennial Parade:** A new parade celebrating 100 years of Disney magic, featuring all your favorite characters, stunning floats, and an uplifting soundtrack.
- **Special Shows:** Enjoy limited time shows and performances that pay tribute to Disney's rich history and beloved stories.
- **Anniversary Merchandise:** Collect exclusive anniversary themed merchandise, including clothing, pins, and souvenirs that commemorate this historic milestone.
- **Decorations:** The entire resort will be adorned with special decorations celebrating 100 years of Disney, creating a festive and nostalgic atmosphere.

Attending these seasonal events and festivities adds an extra layer of excitement and magic to your Disneyland Paris experience. Be sure to check the park's schedule and plan your visit around these special times to make the most of your trip.

Camping at Disneyland Paris | Top Campsites, Parking Options & Regulations

Disneyland Paris is a fantastic holiday destination for kids and those young at heart. Just 45 minutes from Paris, it offers a magical experience filled with entertainment. While the resort boasts various luxurious hotels, a unique camping experience near Disneyland Paris is also available.

Though Disneyland Paris doesn't allow camping onsite, there are facilities for camper parking with specific rules to follow.

Rules of Camping options you will find close by;

Camper Parking Facilities & Rules at Disneyland Paris

Parking for Campers

Campervans can park in Disneyland Paris: Guest Parking area for a daily rate of €45. Please note that the guidelines below must be followed:

- Vehicles with trailers or caravans aren't permitted in Guest Parking.

- Vehicle size must fit within standard bus dimensions.
- A dated receipt will be issued at the Toll Plaza and must be renewed daily.
- Vehicle washing, oil changes, or lubrication aren't allowed in Guest Parking.

General parking rules apply, including no setup of tables or chairs.
Campsites Near Disneyland Paris

Although camping is not available within Disneyland Paris, there are plenty of scenic campsites nearby, providing a peaceful retreat with convenient access to the theme park.

The International de Jablines.: Just a 20minute drive from Disneyland Paris, this campsite offers beach access and beautiful scenery. You can set up a tent, stay in a camper, or rent an onsite cottage. Biking, horseback riding, and water sports are among the activities.

- A daily shuttle service to Disneyland Paris is available.
- Distance from Disneyland Paris: 12 km
- Opens: 30 March to 2 November 2024
- Working Hours: 8 am 12 pm; 2 pm 7 pm
- Address: Base de Loisirs de, 77450 Jablines, France

The Caravaning Des 4 Vents.

This pet friendly site is a 25minute drive from Disneyland Paris, where you can park a mobile home or pitch a tent. Enjoy local attractions, medieval castles, and onsite dining options.

- Distance from Disneyland Paris: 22 km
- Open: 20 March to 1 November 2024
- Hours: 9 am 10 pm
- Address: 22 Rue de Beauregard, 77610 CrèvecoeurenBrie, Île de France, France

Camping near Disneyland Paris Camping Fredland: Ideal for families, this site features play areas, two pools, and water slides. Accommodations range from mobile homes to treehouses, with amenities like dishwashers, AC, and laundry facilities.

- Distance from Disneyland Paris: 19 km
- Open YearRound
- Hours of 9 am to 1 pm and 2 pm to 7 pm.
- Address: 77220 TournanenBrie, France; Parc de Combreux

Camping near Disneyland Paris Campsite Le Chêne Gris

Set in the Grand Morin Valley, this site is surrounded by greenery. It offers indoor and outdoor pools and activities like horseback riding and canoeing. There are tents and mobile homes with water and electricity.

- Distance from Disneyland Paris: 25 km

- Open: 29 March to 27 October 2024
- Hours: 9 am 1 pm; 3 pm 7 pm
- Location: Pommeuse, France 77515, 24 Place de la gare de Faremoutiers

Camping near Disneyland Paris Le Parc de Paris Campsite: For a luxurious camping experience, this site offers fully furnished mobile homes and a VIP package that includes breakfast delivery. Minigolf, ziplining, an upscale restaurant, and an online grocery store are available.

- Distance from Disneyland Paris: 25 km
- Open YearRound
- Hours: 8:30 am 8:30 pm
- The address is 77410 Villevaudé, France, 24 Rue Adèle Claret.

Camping near Disneyland Paris Camping Le Soleil De Crécy
Less than 20 minutes from Disneyland Paris, this campsite offers mobile homes, tent spaces, and a discount for Disney pass holders. Amenities include indoor and outdoor pools and a kids' club.

- Distance from Disneyland Paris: 16 km
- Open: 15 March to 31 October 2024
- Address: Rte de Serbonne, 77580 CrécylaChapelle, France
- Explore these campsites for a memorable camping experience close to the magic of Disneyland Paris!

Disneyland Paris Theme Park Rules

Disneyland Paris offers a magical experience for guests of all ages but has established a comprehensive set of rules to ensure a safe, enjoyable environment for everyone. Here's an overview of the key regulations across different areas of the park, from entry requirements to facilities for children and individuals with disabilities.

Disneyland Paris Theme Park Rules

1. Entry Regulations: A security check is conducted at entry. Visitors should avoid bringing items such as alcoholic beverages, glass containers, selfie sticks, and weapons (or objects resembling them). Remotecontrolled toys and drones are also prohibited.

2. Dress Code: Clothing should be familyfriendly and appropriate for a theme park. Capes, masks (for those over 12), and accessories that can interfere with security are restricted, and clothes dragging on the floor are not allowed.

3. Ticket Rules: Valid tickets must be presented at the entrance, and visitors must retain them throughout their stay. Entry and exit are allowed throughout the day with a hand stamp or approval from park staff.

4. Luggage Restrictions: Large bags over 55cm x 40cm x 25cm aren't allowed inside, while smaller bags may be permitted in the park but not inside attractions.

5. Transport Limitations: Motorized vehicles, bicycles, and roller skates are not allowed. Personal mobility devices are allowed for visitors with disabilities, provided they meet specific safety criteria.

6. Pet Policy: Only certified assistance animals are permitted, provided they remain on a leash, and medical proof is required.

7. Child Safety: Children under 12 must be accompanied by an adult over 15. Age verification is conducted for attractions, and some rides may be restricted for children under one year.

8. Conduct and Cleanliness: All visitors are expected to maintain a respectful environment and avoid engaging in disruptive behavior. Eating, drinking, and using flash photography are discouraged in attractions and theaters.

9. Health Precautions: Guests with health concerns, including pregnant women and individuals with disabilities, are advised to inform staff about any specific needs or restrictions.

10. Prohibited Commercial Activity: Selling items or distributing pamphlets without authorization is not allowed.

11. Smoking: Smoking is only permitted in designated areas, including for electronic cigarettes.

Special Services for Guests

Disneyland Paris offers various services for guests with special needs, families with young children, and pet owners to ensure a convenient experience.

1. Services for Guests with Disabilities: The park is equipped with accessibility features, including wheelchair access in restaurants and shops. Priority cards are available, and support from Cast Members is provided for navigating attractions and theaters.

2. Disney Express Hotel Luggage Service: Guests staying at a Disney hotel can check in and drop off their luggage at the Disney Express counter, located at the MarnelaVallée/Chessy train station.

3. Children's Amenities: The park offers kidfriendly services such as healthy meal options (Disney Check), babysitting services, pushchair rentals, baby care centers, and the Rider Switch system for parents. Additionally, there are dedicated meeting points for lost children and a First Aid center located on Main Street, U.S.A.

These services and rules help Disneyland Paris maintain a safe and enjoyable environment for all visitors, making it one of the most accessible and familyfriendly theme parks globally.

Disneyland Paris Parade Highlights

The parades at Disneyland Paris offer guests unforgettable experiences with vibrant displays, music, and beloved Disney characters. Here's a closer look at some of the key parades that bring Disney dreams to life.

Disneyland Paris Parade Highlights

1. Disney Electrical Sky Parade

Description: This nighttime show features synchronized drones creating spectacular visuals in the sky. Inspired by the iconic Main Street Electrical Parade, it presents dazzling colors and Disney shapes that appear above the Sleeping Beauty Castle.

Duration: Approximately 8 minutes

Show Times: Daily, after sunset (varies by season)

Dates: 8 January 30 September

Location: Above the Sleeping Beauty Castle

2. A Million Splashes of Colour

Description: A lively daytime parade with Disney and Pixar favorites like Mickey, Timon, Joy, and Mirabel. This parade celebrates diversity, joy, and music with energetic dancing, colorful costumes, and singalong tunes.

Duration: Approximately 20 minutes

Show Times: Multiple times daily (varies by season)

Dates: 10th February to 30th September

Location: Just in front of the Sleeping Beauty Castle by Central Plaza.

3. Disney Stars on Parade

Description: Set in the Walt Disney Studios Park, this is a unique meetandgreet experience rather than a traditional parade. Characters like Mickey and Pixar stars stroll down Hollywood Boulevard, giving fans a chance to meet, take photos, and gather autographs.

Duration: Throughout the day, depending on character availability

Show Times: No fixed schedule, happening throughout the day

Location: Hollywood Boulevard, Walt Disney Studios Park

These parades not only bring Disney magic to life but also offer a perfect way for families to connect, celebrate, and create memories together in the enchanting world of Disneyland Paris.

MY DISNEY EXPRIENCES!

DAY/DATES   **EVENTS**

MY PERSONAL NOTES!

ISBN 9798300000639